"I'LL HAVE MY CHILD BACK" THE SOJOURNER TRUTH STORY

BY

RASHID A. HAMZAH

First Edition

Hamzah Publishing
www.hamzahpublishing.net
Albany, New York

SOJOURNER TRUTH
CA. 1797 — NOV. 26, 1883

FAMOUS SLAVE OF ULSTER COUNTY, BORN IN HURLEY, N.Y. THOUGH ILLITERATE, THIS WOMAN OF INDOMITABLE CHARACTER AND INTELLECT LEFT HER INDELIBLE MARK AS AN ELOQUENT CONDEMNER OF SLAVERY. FROM THIS COURT, BY WINNING HER LAWSUIT - THE FIRST EVER WON BY A BLACK PARENT - SHE SAVED HER SON FROM SLAVERY IN ALABAMA. A STAUNCH ABOLITIONIST AND A FERVENT CHAMPION OF HUMAN RIGHTS, SHE MET PRESIDENT LINCOLN AND SUBSEQUENTLY SERVED AS ADVISOR AT FREEDOM VILLAGE IN VIRGINIA. HER OWN WORDS EXPLAIN HER TRIUMPH: "I TALK TO GOD AND GOD TALKS TO ME."

PLAQUE IN FRONT OF ULSTER COUNTY COURTHOUSE KINGSTON, NEW YORK

"I'LL HAVE MY CHILD BACK"

The Sojourner Truth Story

By: Rashid A. Hamzah

SPECIAL THANKS TO:

Scott and Mary Coon, and the staff of the Albany Public Library, who tolerated my unending questions about computers. Bethany and all my family and friends who gave me both moral and financial support through out this long process. My cousins Mark Toney and Blaine Gibbs for standing out in the rain and getting the photographs for me. Paul Stewart who helped me with the lay out of the book, and his son, (you could have came in and had tea and watched the game.) Also to Abdullah Waduh for his patients.

Dedication

This book is dedicated to the memory of my mother,
Henrietta M. Morton,
I love you and I miss you.

The Old Home of Sojourner Truth

SOJOURNER TRUTH'S CHURCH STREET HOME BATTLECREEK, MICHIGAN

Sitting, staring out the window, watching the countryside pass by, I realized I wasn't looking forward to my interview with Sojourner Truth, unlike the first time I interviewed her some thirty years ago in Akron, Ohio, when I was a new reporter on my first assignment. Then, I stayed true to everyday white male prejudices and beliefs. I felt a woman, especially a nigra ex-slave woman, didn't have anything worthwhile to say that a white man needed to listen to. How wrong I was. Not only did Sojourner Truth change the course of history, this eloquent, inspirational woman taught me we all have a voice in life that makes up the melody of the human experience.

Today it wasn't silly prejudices or dumb beliefs that caused my reluctance. Age, time and illness had become the only obstacles Sojourner wasn't able to over come. I knew she was dying, and this could be my last visit with her. The other passengers on the train were celebrating the holidays. I was the only one on the train that knew one of America's greatest voices would soon be silent. It saddened me.

When I arrived at the Battle Creek, Michigan train station, I decided to walk to Sojourner's home. Although it was a cold, late November day, I didn't notice the weather. As I walked to the door of the little house, Sojourner's daughter, Sophie, greeted me.

"Morton, I'm glad you could come. Mother will be happy to see you," she said.

"Hello Sophie. How is she today? Is she comfortable?" I asked.

"She's tired and ready to go home. But she's been waiting to see you. You know you're her favorite boy," Sophie smiled and walked into Sojourner's bedroom.

Sophie returned and motioned for me to enter the room. Entering, I expected to see a frail, bed-ridden woman waiting to die. Instead, I was greeted by Sojourner's smile.

"My little man has come to visit Ole Sojourner," she said. "God bless you. How are you and your family?"

I'm 50 years old and she still calls me her little man.

"I'm doing fine Miss Sojourner. My wife sends her love and God's Blessings to you. Isabelle, Betsey, James and little Peter also sends their love," I replied.

Sojourner had such an impact on my life, my wife and I had named our children after her birth name, her mother and father names, and her beloved son's name.

Sojourner told me to sit down in the chair next to her bed and told me the news of the day. She said we were moving into the 'special times,' as she would always put it. She wished she could see the 1900s, but was tired and happy to be going home.

As she spoke to me, my mind slipped back to 1851 Akron, Ohio, the first time I met with her. Back then as she entered the Assembly Hall, the crowd rudely began to yell at her. I was also guilty of rude behavior. Even then, however, I noticed something regal about this tall, muscular woman. She didn't allow the crowd to intimidate her. She had a look of determination on her face. She had a message to deliver and no one, or anything was going to stop her. It was then I realized I should be quiet and listen to what she had to say.

As her tall, muscular figure regally walked up the aisle of the meeting hall, the crowd began to shout, "What's she doing here? This has nothing to do with slavery. We're talking about women's rights." But that didn't stop her. Nothing stopped her.

When I sat down and spoke with Sojourner, she smiled at me and said, "You're not happy having to talk to Ole Sojourner, are you?"

"Let's just do this interview," I replied.

"Come sit down, my Little Man, and let me tell you my story," she said.

"When I walked up that aisle I began to think to myself, look at all them people, coming to hear this talk. I knew I'd traveled a long way to get here to talk. Wasn't talkin about miles, talkin about living. Didn't think I was going to make it. I didn't think I was going to make it at all. God was with me. God was always with me. That's where I get my strength. And now I've come with what God has given me, 'The Truth,' " she continued.

Sojourner didn't let the crowd bother her. She walked to the front of the meeting hall and sat down on the stairs of the stage. This meeting in Akron, Ohio was organized to discuss the question of the equality of women to men. Several male speakers had expressed their opinions why men were superior to women. Sojourner Truth was not swayed by their arguments. She too was a very persuasive and dynamic speaker. Her sincere, eloquent abolitionist message moved her listeners. John Dumont, a slave owner who once owned Sojourner Truth, became an abolitionist through the persuasion of this woman of strong character and intellect.

"Master Dumont was a good master as slave owners go." Sojourner told me.

"He worked us hard, but he didn't beat us like the other owners did."

Early in 1826 Dumont had made a promise to Sojourner Truth. New York had passed a law saying that the slaves were to get their freedom on the Forth of July 1827. Dumont told Sojourner that if she would do well and be faithful, and if she worked hard for him throughout the planting season and the harvest season, he'd give her the freedom papers early.

"I worked hard. I remembered my Mawmaw Bett told me never to lie or steal, and to always obey your master," She told me. "I followed Mawmaw Bett's lessons good."

Sojourner had worked hard, but she had two obstacles to overcome. She had given birth to her daughter Sophie, and she had cut her hand while working. The cut was bad and it got infected. She still worked hard and believed she had done her part to earn her freedom, as agreed.

"As we came upon July 4, Master Dumont told me because I had cut my hand and had Sophie, I hadn't done my work and he wanted me to stay for another year," Sojourner said. "I told Master Dumont I had done my part and had earned my freedom."

"Dumont was wrong. I had worked hard, even with my cut hand. Even after having Sophie, I worked hard. The other slaves got mad at me because I worked more than the men. I earned my freedom and nothing would stop me from taking it," Sojourner said.

After the harvest was done, Sojourner decided it was time to take what she had earned, her freedom. So early one morning, just before sunrise Sojourner packed up Sophie and the provisions she had coming to her and walked away from Dumont's farm through the woods to her Freedom.

"I was scared. I didn't know where I was going. But I knew where I couldn't stay," she said.

"I remembered the Quaker Levi Rowe, and how much against slavery he was, 'It is not right anyone should be a slave,' he would say. So I went to his home to get his help. Mr. Levi had taken ill. He was in bed as if he was waiting for death to come and take him away," she said.

"Levi apologized for not being able to get up and for not being able to help me. He told me to go see a Quaker family Van Wagenen and they maybe able to help me."

Sojourner told me how she washed Levi and cleaned his home. She cooked him a meal and gave him comfort in his final hours.

"Levi said to me, 'God's Blessings be with you Belle' and offered me some money for helping him. I didn't know anything about money, never had to use it before and didn't understand why you took money for showing human kindness. So I took the Blessings and told Levi to keep his money. I know I'm better with what comes from God than what comes from man," Sojourner said.

Sojourner then went to the home of the Van Wagenen family to ask for their help. When she arrived at the home Isaac and Maria Van Wagenen, she told them about Levi and his illness. She told them how he had said they maybe able to help her. Sojourner then told the Van Wagenen family about Dumont's broken promise of Freedom.

The Quakers were strict abolitionists; they always were ready to help slaves get their freedom. The Van Wagenen family welcomed the chance to help Sojourner and her daughter Sophie. They opened their home to them.

The next morning Sojourner and the Van Wagenens heard horses approaching the house. Sojourner knew it was Dumont coming after her.

"I worked hard for you. You broke the promise. I earned my Freedom, so I'm taking it. I didn't run away from you, I walked to my Freedom." Sojourner boldly said to Dumont.

Dumont argued with Sojourner for a while. He told her, her cut hand and the birth of baby Sophie had slowed her and she owed him one more year. He said it would cost him money if she left now. The Van Wagenen family offers to pay $25.00 for Dumont's loses, he reluctantly agreed. Isabelle Dumont now becomes Isabelle Van Wagenen, a Free Woman.

During the next year, Sojourner worked at the home of the Van Wagenen family, earning a small wage and enjoying her newfound freedom.

In the spring of the following year, households in the county were preparing for the Pinxster. Pinxster, a Dutch word for Pentecost, was a festival, which came fifty days after Easter. It was a weeklong celebration for the slaves in which they didn't have to work. It was filled with festive music and dancing. 1827 was especially festive; Freedom for the slaves in New York was coming. Although already free, Sojourner felt the excitement. Dumont returned to the Van Wagenen home to ask Sojourner if she wanted to spend the Pinxster at his farm. She declined. With Freedom comes choice, something Sojourner was becoming very comfortable with.

When Sojourner left Dumont's farm, all she took was a small bag of provisions and her baby Sophie. Her other children, including her young son Peter, were left under the ownership of Dumont. She feared for their fates, but with freedom for all slaves coming soon, she believed Dumont would keep her children safe.

"My Mama and Papa told me how it pained them to have their children sold off like property. I didn't know how deep the hurt was until my baby Peter was sold off to Solomon Gedney. I didn't know how bad it would get," she said.

I saw Sojourner become deeply solemn as she recalled the events of her fight to get Peter back from Gedney.

Sojourner was told that Peter was with Solomon Gedney to become a gentleman's porter, a type of valet. Soon she found that Gedney had given the boy to Lisa Gedney Fowler to live in Alabama. Mr. Fowler, Lisa's husband, was known to have a bad temper and fits of violent rages. Lisa also feared her husband.

Sojourner wept as she told me the details of the story.

"The slaves in New York were getting their freedom. Slaving in Alabama was hard and white folks there weren't giving it up. I knew my baby was going through some bad times. I knew I had to do something. I just didn't know what," Sojourner said. Sojourner didn't realize at the time how much danger the boy was truly in.

Sojourner went to Dumont's farm to ask why he sold Peter. There she met with Mrs. Dumont. Dumont's wife didn't understand the fuss Sojourner was making.

"Ugh! A fine fuss to make about a little nigra! Why, haven't you as many of 'em left as you can see to? Making such a hullabaloo about the neighborhood, and all for a paltry nigra child," she angrily shouted at Sojourner.

Sojourner calmly turned to her and replied, "I'll have my baby back again."

"Have your child again?" Mrs. Dumont said with contempt. "How can you get him? And what have you to support him with if you could? Have you any money?"

"No," answered Sojourner. "I have no money, but what we get comes from God and He has enough to support us. I'll have my child again."

As she told me the details of the story she said, "When I spoke to Mistress Dumont that way, I felt so tall within. I felt as if the power of a nation was in me."

When Sojourner left Mrs. Dumont, she went to the Gedney farm and spoke with Solomon and Lisa Gedney' mother.

"Why have you sent my baby to Alabama?" Sojourner said to Mrs. Gedney.

Annoyed at Sojourner's boldness, Mrs. Gedney replied to her, "Is your child better than my child? My child has also gone to Alabama and yours is gone to live with her, to have enough of everything. He will be treated like a gentleman." Mrs. Gedney mockingly began to laugh.

Sojourner answered, "Yes, your child, Lisa, has gone there, but she is married. My baby Peter is a slave. He is too little to go so far away from his Mama. Oh, I must have my baby back."

As Sojourner left Gedney's house, she could still hear Mrs. Gedney laughing. She began to pray, "God, You just have to be my Helper. Oh please, show them that You are my Helper."

The Van Wagenen family advised Sojourner about her legal rights and told her she needed to get a lawyer. Sending the boy to Alabama as a slave was illegal in New York State.

"I didn't know about legal this or legal that, laws or lawyers. I just know a baby suppose to be with his Mama and a Mama supposed to be with her baby. God made it that way and no man has the right to undo it." The strength and determination returned to her face as she spoke.

Sojourner traveled to Kingston, New York, where she met Squire Chip. She told him what had happened to her son Peter and she wanted to get him back. Knowing the law regarding slavery in New York, Squire Chip told her to meet with the Grand Jury at the Kingston Courthouse.

Having no knowledge of the law, courts, or the Grand Jury, Sojourner didn't understand what a Grand Jury was or did. She though the Grand Jury was a man. She saw several men dressed in suits and asked, "Are you the Grand Jury?" She then asked another man, "Are you the Grand Jury?"

Sojourner was told to go to the third floor of the courthouse, there she saw a finely dressed man with a smile. She walked over to him and asked, "Sir you look mighty grand, are you the Grand Jury?"

Mockingly he asked her, "And what can I do for you?"

Sojourner told him how Solomon Gedney had sent her son Peter to Alabama as a slave. The man understood the seriousness of the problem and listened intently to her plea. Squire Chip joined them and they proceeded to the Grand Jury Room.

Squire Chip and Sojourner walked into the jury room and she spoke to the Grand Jury. "Solomon Gedney sent my baby, Peter, to Alabama as a slave. The law said that is wrong. Please sir, I want him back."

A juror asked her, "What do you know about the law?"

"I know Master Gedney wasn't supposed to send my baby south. That's all I need to know," she replied. "I'm not asking you to do anything special for me. Just make Solomon Gedney obey your laws and send my baby back to me. God will do the rest."

"How do we even know the child is hers?" asked another juror.

"I carried that baby inside of me. And fed him from my breasts. He is mine! Solomon Gedney had nothing to do with that," she answered.

Squire Chip placed Sojourner's hand on a bible and asked, "Would you be willing to swear the child you speak of is your son?"

Sojourner answered, "Oh, yes, I swear he is."

"What's the use of making her swear? She can't understand what it means," added a juror.

"It will satisfy the law," replied Squire Chip. He then led

Sojourner out of the room, while the jurors debated the case.

"How can we rule in favor of a nigra woman against Solomon Gedney?" one juror said.

"He did break the law," replied another.

"Gedney will destroy us," added a third juror.

Squire Chip reminded them about New York's law regarding commerce in slavery.

"You don't have to tell us about the Law, we helped write the Law," shouted the third juror.

The judge was quietly sitting in the back of the room listening to the deliberations. He slowly stood up, cleared his throat, and began,

"This isn't about black or white, male or female, rich or poor. And it surely isn't about Solomon Gedney. This is a matter of Law.

"What is the need to have Laws, if we let someone break them just because he is a rich white man?

"Rich white men are protected by the power of their

money. Laws protect the rest of us. Gedney broke the Law, now he must pay the consequence.

"And we will pay the consequence of Solomon Gedney," added the third juror.

"Then that's what we'll do. The Law is the Law," replied the judge, he then sat down.

The jurors agreed to give Sojourner a Writ to give to the constable in New Paltz. Sojourner returned to the jury room where Squire Chip explained the Writ to her.

"This is a Writ. Take it to the constable in New Paltz and he will give it to Solomon Gedney. It will make him give you your son back," Squire Chip told her.

"The nigra doesn't even know what a Writ is," shouted the third juror.

Sojourner turned to him smiled and said; "It's what will bring my baby Peter back to me. That's all I need to know. That's all that's important."

With the Writ and baby Sophie in hand, Sojourner walked the nine miles from Kingston to New Paltz and handed the Writ to the constable.

"What's this?" the constable asked.

"It's to get my baby back from Solomon Gedney," Sojourner answered. "The judge in Kingston told me to give it to you and you will give it to Master Gedney. That will get my Peter home where he belongs. With his Mama."

"Nothing makes Gedney do what he doesn't want to do," replied the constable.

"God will," Sojourner quipped as she handed him the Writ. "So will the Law."

Weeks, months and over a year passed and Peter still was not home. Sojourner became disheartened. All the people, including Squire Chip, had gotten tired of her constant inquiries about Peter. One evening, while sitting near the courthouse in Kingston, Sojourner, stretched her arms to the sky, cried out, "God, are You tired of me too? Send someone who will show me some good. I need help in this matter."

A freed male slave Sojourner knew called out to her, "Hello there. How are you getting on with your boy? Did they give him up to you yet?"

"William, how are you doing?" Sojourner replied. "Did you get your freedom yet?"

"Yes. I live up in the Eagle's Nest and work down in the Rondout," he told her. "How's things with Peter?"

"Not good, William. He's not home and now people are getting tired of me," she said. "There's no one left to help."

William pointed across the street, and said, "Do you see that stone house over yonder?" Sojourner looked across the street at the house. "Lawyer Romeyn lives there. Go see him and tell him about your case. He'll help you."

Sojourner got up and started towards the house. William said to her as she walked across the street, "Belle, it's a good thing what you're doing. You're a strong woman and when you fight for what's right, we all feel everything going to be good with us. Don't give Lawyer Romeyn any peace until he agrees to help you."

William watched as Sojourner walked to the stone house.

Lawyer Romeyn was a young local lawyer, just starting his practice. He strongly believed laws must be obeyed. Sojourner, passionately, told him her case. Lawyer Romeyn knew she had a case and agreed to help her.

"If you can bring me five dollars to pay a constable, I'll get your son back to you within twenty-four hours.

Sojourner collected more than the five dollars, Lawyer Romeyn had asked for, from her Quaker friends. She returned to Lawyer Romeyn's office and gave him all the money she collected.

After Sojourner gave the money to Lawyer Romeyn, he told her to return to his office in twenty-four hours. Sojourner didn't understand time or how to count hours. Impatiently she returned to the office in a short period.

"Lawyer Romeyn, that woman is here again," his servant called out.

"I know day and night. Planting time and harvest time. Hours and minutes don't mean anything to me," Sojourner said.

Lawyer Romeyn told Sojourner to come back in the morning, and she would find her son there. He told her to find lodging with her Quaker friends.

Sojourner went to the home of her Quaker friends. A woman answered the door and after Sojourner told her the story of her son, the woman took her to a room with a tall bed in it.

"You can sleep here," the woman told Sojourner.

"I was scared when she left me alone with the bed. I never slept in a real bed, so it never came in my head to sleep on it. So I just camped under it. Me and Sophie slept pretty good that night there on the floor under that bed," Sojourner said.

The next morning, Sojourner returned to the office of Lawyer Romeyn. She noticed he had a frown on his face.

"Belle, I've seen your son. He said he had no mother or any family here. You need to meet me at the courthouse to identify him yourself," Romeyn said.

Later that afternoon, Sojourner went to the courthouse and met with Lawyer Romeyn and together they went to the judge's chambers. There stood Solomon Gedney, behind him was Peter, clinging to Gedney's leg.

Sojourner called out to Peter, but the boy didn't move. Kneeling down, Sojourner once again called out to Peter. Again the frightened boy didn't answer his mother.

"This is not the boy's mother. You made me go through this for nothing," Gedney angrily said.

The judge looked at the boy and then asked Sojourner,

**ULSTER COUNTY COURTHOUSE
KINGSTON, NEW YORK**

"Is this your baby?"

"Yes," she answered without hesitation.

"Are you sure?" the judge asked.

"I carried that boy inside of me, and fed him with milk

from my breast. I know my baby," she said sharply.

"This nigra doesn't know what she is talking about. The boy doesn't know who she is. I'm taking the boy and going home. Thanks for wasting my time," Gedney angrily said.

The judge looked at Gedney and said, "You're not going anywhere. Sit down."

The judge called Peter over to him. The boy hesitated but the judge persuaded Peter to come to him.

"Do you know this woman?" the judge asked Peter.

"No sir," Peter answered.

Gedney started to get up. The judge just glared at him. Gedney sat down and remained quiet.

The judge asked Peter, "Do you know what the truth is?"

"Yes sir," Peter replied.

"Did your Mama teach you that?" the judge asked.

Peter looked towards Gedney.

"Don't look at him, look at me," the judge told the boy.

Peter turned back towards the judge.

Noticing a large gash on his head, the judge asked, "How did you get this cut on your head?"

Peter nervously lowered his head and said, "Master Fowler's horse kicked me."

The judge pulled Peter to him and hugged him tightly then said, "No one will ever hurt you like that again. Not Gedney. Not Fowler. Not anybody. Your Mama taught you to tell the Truth. That was a good thing. She must love you very much. Make her proud of you. Tell me the Truth. Do you know this woman?"

Peter looked to his mother and said, "Yes sir."

"Is this your Mama?" the judge asked.

Again, Peter tried to look towards Gedney.

"Don't look at him," the judge shouted.

Peter looked toward his mother. She smiled. Peter then said, "It looks like her."

The judge again asked the boy, "Son is this your Mama?"

Peter rushed into the arms of Sojourner and said, "Yes sir this is my Mama."

Sojourner and Peter hugged and kissed one another as though they would never let each other go.

Gedney stormed out of the judge's chambers. As he left he shouted, "You haven't heard the last of this."

The judge says to himself, "Probably not! Probably not!"

As Sojourner held her baby again in her arms, she noticed the scars from the beatings the little boy had taken from Fowler.

"Master Fowler whipped and kicked and beat me," Peter told his mother. "Sometimes I'd crawl under the stoop to hide, blood all over me. One time Master Fowler found me there and dragged me out and had his horse kick me."

"What did Miss Lisa do when they treated you this badly?"

Sojourner asked. "Mama, she would tell me everything would be all right, that I'd be home with you soon," Peter said. "And she would clean and grease my sores when everybody was asleep."

Sojourner looked up and shouted, "What kind of animals are you people? He is only a baby, and you beat him like you would a man. I curse you, double what you have done to my baby."

She would come to regret her words when she learned Lisa Gedney Fowler was murdered, in a fit of rage, by her husband.

"I didn't mean to wish death on anyone," she said solemnly.

I don't think Sojourner realized the importance of what she did. She had changed the course of history. If you asked her about it she'd tell you she did what a mother was suppose to do.

"After I won in court, they told me it was the first time a black ex-slave woman got her child back from slavery. They said it was historical. Well I don't know about historical, I just know God puts babies with Mamas and no man's suppose to come between it," she said.

I remember she told me how she became Sojourner Truth. "It was time for me to go about God's work. I knew the old names given to me in slavery would not do for God's pilgrim. I began to pray, 'Oh God, give me a name, a good name for your servant.' And when my only Master, God, sent my name to me, my heart filled with joy. I've always had the name of my masters. Now God, The Truth, was my only true Master. And He was sending me traveling throughout the land with His Message. That is my name, Sojourner Truth, the lone traveler with God's Message," Sojourner beamed with joy as she told me this story.

Traveled with her message she did. I was happy fate brought us together. As I watched her sit on the stage in Ohio, the crowd rudely shouted at her. I thought she would not dare to stand up on the stage and speak. I was wrong. Her speech changed my life and beliefs forever.

Sojourner was called to the podium. As she walked up the stairs, the crowd became louder. Sojourner in a low soft voice, which rose in intensity during the speech, began,

"Well children, where there is so much racket, there must be something out of kilter. That something is the control of women and blacks by white men. The supporters of this unequal order will be in a fix pretty soon."

As the crowd began to quiet, she pointed to a man sitting in the audience, and continued,

"That man over there, that man says that women need to be helped into carriages and lifted over ditches and have the best places everywhere. Nobody ever helps me into carriages or over mud puddles or gives me any best place!"

In a loud voice, which roared like thunder, Sojourner said, "And aren't I a Woman? Look at me! Look at my arms!"

Sojourner rolled up the sleeves of her dress and held out her muscular arms, than said,

"I have plowed and planted and gathered into barns and no man could out work me. And aren't I a woman?

"I could work as much and eat as much as a man, when I could get it. And took the lash! And aren't I a woman?"

Sojourner placed her hands over her stomach, and in a solemn voice said, "I have borne five children and saw them sold off as slaves and when I cried out with a mother's grief, none but God heard me. And aren't I a woman?"

Sojourner looked out to the crowd at another man, and continued,
"That man talks about this thing in the head. What's that

they call it? Intellect! Yea, that's it. What's intellect got to do with women's rights or black folks' rights? If my cup won't hold but a pint and yours hold a quart, wouldn't you be mean not to let me have my little half measure full? That little man in the black suit there says women can't have as much rights as men because Jesus wasn't a woman."

Sojourner stood with her arms stretched out and said,

"Where do Jesus son of Mary come from? Where did he come from? From God and a woman. Man had nothing to do with him."

Sojourner turned and confronted a minister, who spoke about Eve and the original sin, she continued,

"If the first woman God ever made was strong enough to turn the world upside down all alone, these women together ought to be able turn it back and get it right side up again. And now that they are asking to do it, the men better let them!"

Sojourner bent over to pick up her sunbonnet, stood up and said, "Obliged to you for hearing me. Now Ole Sojourner hasn't anything more to say."

Sojourner Truth did have much more to say. She carried

her message to the people into her eighties. But now her work was coming to an end. I sat there and listened to Sojourner tell me how we are certainly heading to new times. I got the sense that, yes the woman we knew as Isabelle Hardenburg, Isabelle Neely, Isabelle Dumont and Isabelle Van Wagenen, was about to pass on from this life. The spirit, however, of Sojourner Truth would always live on, not only with me, but also with us all.

As I got ready to leave, I bent over to kiss her forehead, as I always did. She reached for my face and kissed me on my cheek. It was the first time in the thirty years I had known her that she ever did that. She looked at me smiled and said, "God didn't give me the chance to see my son, Peter, grow to be a man. But He blessed me with seeing you grow up to be a fine and honorable man. And with a Mother's hope, I would like to think Peter would have grown up to be just like you."

When I started to leave I began to tell her how much I loved her and how much of a mother she had been to me. She put her finger to my lips to shush me, smiled and said, "I know." She lay back down and went to sleep. It was the last time I saw her alive. I miss my visits with Sojourner, but she is still very much alive in my heart. I hope this story will bring this incredible woman's spirit alive in your heart.

SOJOURNER TRUTH'S GRAVESITE
BATTLECREEK, MICHIGAN

Her signature

Click to enlarge

A copy of her signature, reproduced on a wall in the College Library from an 1880 autograph.

APENDEX:

Original Hymns Authored by Sojourner Truth

<u>I AM PLEADING FOR MY PEOPLE</u>

I AM PLEADING FOR MY PEOPLE
A POOR, DOWNTRODDEN RACE,
WHO DWELL IN FREEDOM'S BOASTED
LAND, WITH NO ABIDING PLACE.

WHILST I BEAR UPON MY BODY
THE SCARS OF MANY A GASH
I AM PLEADING FOR MY PEOPLE
WHO GROAN BENEATH THE LASH?

I AM PLEADING FOR THE MOTHERS
WHO GAZE IN WILD DESPAIR
UPON THE HATED AUCTION-BLOCK,
AND SEE THEIR CHILDREN THERE.

I PITY THE SLAVE MOTHER

O, SLAVE MOTHER, HOPE! SEE-THE NATION IS SHAKING!
THE ARM OF THE LORD IS AWAKE TO THY WRONG!
THE SLAVEHOLDER'S HEART NOW WITH TERROR IS QUAKING,
SALVATION AND MERCY TO HEAVEN BELONG!
REJOICE, O REJOICE! FOR THE CHILD THOU ART REARING! MAY
ONE DAY LIFT UP ITS UNMANACLEDFORM,
WHILE HOPE, TO THY HEART, LIKE THE RAINBOW SO CHEERING,
IS BORN, LIKE THE RAINBOW, MID TEMPEST AND STORM.

I PITY THE SLAVE MOTHER, CAREWORN AND WEARY,
WHO SIGHS AS SHE PRESSES HER BABE TO HER BREAST;
I LAMENT HER SAD FATE, ALL SO HOPELESS AND DREARY,
I LAMENT FOR HER WOES, AND HER WRONGS UNREDRESSED.
O WHO CAN IMAGINE HER HEART'S DEEPEMOTION,
AS SHE THINKS OF HER CHILDREN ABOUT TO BE SOLD;
YOU MAY PICTURE THE BOUNDS OF THE ROCK-GIRDLED OCEAN,
BUT THE GRIEF OF THAT MOTHER CAN NEVER BE TOLD.

After his young wife died with cancer in 1987, Rashid A. Hamzah was left with the task of raising their then 4 year old son Muhammed. In December 1991 Rashid and his son moved to Kingston, New York to care for his elderly mother. This was the beginning of his quest for Truth. When his son choose Sojourner Truth as a Black History Month assignment, Rashid took Muhammed to see the play "A Woman Called Truth" and became fascinated with this courageous woman. "I'll Have My Child Back" The Sojourner Truth Story is the bases for his play of the same name. Mr. Hamzah, whose background is in television production, is in the process of writing a screenplay and is planning to bring this story to the big screen.

www.ingramcontent.com/pod-product-compliance
Lightning Source LLC
Chambersburg PA
CBHW080948050426
42337CB00055B/4730